SHORT WALKS

Warwickshire
Pubs

Richard Shurey

COUNTRYSIDE BOOKS
NEWBURY, BERKSHIRE

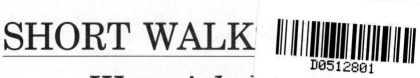

COUNTRYSIDE BOOKS
3 Catherine Road
Newbury, Berkshire

ISBN 1 85306 438 6

Designed by Mon Mohan
Cover illustration by Colin Doggett
Photographs and maps by the author

Produced through MRM Associates Ltd., Reading
Printed by Woolnough Bookbinding Ltd.,
Irthlingborough

Contents

Publisher's Note

We hope that you obtain considerable enjoyment from this book; great care has been taken in its preparation. However, changes of landlord and actual closures are sadly not uncommon. Likewise, although at the time of publication all routes followed public rights of way or permitted paths, diversion orders can be made and permissions withdrawn.

We cannot of course be held responsible for such diversion orders and any inaccuracies in the text which result from these or any other changes to the routes nor any damage which might result from walkers trespassing on private property. However, we are anxious that all details covering the walks and the pubs are kept up to date and would therefore welcome information from readers which would be relevant to future editions.

Area map showing locations of the walks.

Introduction

I was delighted when the publisher asked me to complete another volume of walks based on Warwickshire pubs following the success of the first book. By having to restrict the number in that book, many wonderful pubs were excluded and they have now found a rightful place in this companion volume.

Seeking out the pubs was also a fine opportunity to discover the beautiful countryside of the county which produced two of England's finest literary figures. Both Shakespeare and George Eliot drew inspiration from the scenery, customs and folklore of 'leafy' Warwickshire.

This is a county which has many pretty villages and a traditional, essential feature of any rural community is the pub. Sadly, of course, many pubs have been lost to us during recent years because of changing social patterns. Most of these hostelries were too slow to appreciate that the old type of pub with its rather spartan features was no longer widely acceptable. Those that were willing to undergo the difficult (and often costly) changes have thrived and contributed much to pleasant outings into the county's quiet and lovely byways.

Whereas families and children were often discouraged (mainly let it be said because of archaic licensing laws) they are now invariably welcomed because of the increased trade they bring. Special menus, play areas and family rooms are becoming common.

The walks are all of modest length but long enough to generate a thirst and an appetite. The routes are along quiet lanes and footpaths – the county has done much in recent years to clear and mark the rights of way. Farmers and landowners increasingly appreciate that it is better to welcome walkers along unambiguous tracks.

The sketch maps should be sufficient (read with the text of the walk) to follow the routes without difficulty. However, it adds interest to the walk and indicates possible short-cuts if the relevant 1:50 000 Landranger Series map is carried.

The pubs selected are spread throughout the length of Warwickshire. In the north there is pleasant countryside still, although the region is undergoing constant pressure from the need for more highways and modern 'green field' industrial estates.

The middle of the county is the area which was once the great Forest of Arden so beloved by Shakespeare. Many of the trees were felled in the 18th century for iron smelting. However, many small tracts of woodland remain and like the creatures of Shakespeare's fancy, we can on our rambles 'fleet the time carelessly as they did in the ancient world'.

South of the river Avon is the Feldon – the open farming country. This has an especial lonely loveliness with patchwork fields which gradually rise towards the south borderlands, into the ironstone ridges like historic Edge Hill and the limestone beauty of the Cotswolds.

This immense variety of scenery ensures that every walk produces new pleasures before that pub meal. Most of the pubs have their own car park but it would, of course, be polite to notify the staff of your intention to use their custom on your return.

With the changed regulations, hours of opening are nowadays under constant review by the pubs. They can be a lot more flexible and extended or curtailed as trade warrants. The times when meals are available are somewhat shorter than the opening hours and it is advisable to check prior to starting the ramble.

Going for a country walk is now by far the most popular pastime; perhaps one attraction is that it allows the family to enjoy undertaking something together. Also no special equipment is required – but do remember there can be mud in the countryside and it is known to rain now and then to ensure our land is green and beautiful. Happy Warwickshire rambling!

Richard Shurey
Spring 1996

① Shuttington
The Wolferstan Arms

You may think that the grey pebble-dash makes this pub look rather dull – do not be deceived! This magnificent and popular hostelry goes out of its way to attract clients, encouraging those who want a quiet meal (with small alcoves for that discreet tête à tête) as well as families (with appealing menus and a magnificent play area).

In this Marston's managed house there is a public bar (with its dartboard and where dogs are allowed) and a large lounge/100-seater restaurant with a most lovely view far across the valley and nature reserve pools. The terrace has this wonderful vista too and barbecue meals are served here during the summer months. There are plenty of benches and tables and this is one of the very rare pubs where bringing one's own sandwiches is not frowned upon.

The old prints on the walls are fascinating – from past days there are views of the area, personalities and tradesmen and an especially interesting poster for the Midlands Miners' Association to remind us that this was once a great area for the extraction of coal. There are tools and memorabilia of the countryman too, including such things as malting tools and gin traps.

The beers available at the Wolferstan Arms (which was named after the landowning family of nearby Statfold Hall and is about two centuries old) are Marston's Pedigree and Bitter plus for variety the current Marston's Head Brewer's Choice. There is also Banks's Mild, together with four lager brands and draught Strongbow and Woodpecker.

The pub does not have a particularly large menu but what you will find are reasonably-priced dishes with several salads such as the prawn and Marie Rose (selected prawns topped with a creamy seafood sauce). In addition there are always the 'specials of the day' attractively chalked on a board near the bar, such as sweet and sour pork and several popular vegetarian dishes.

The opening hours are Monday to Friday 11 am to 2.30 pm and 6 pm to 11 pm. Saturday is the same except the lunchtime closing is at 3 pm. There is all day opening on Sundays from 12 noon.

Telephone: 01827 892238.

How to get there: 3 miles north-east of Tamworth along the B5493 turn right along a lane signed to Shuttington. The pub is at the far end of the village on the right.

Parking: There is a large car park at the rear of the pub.

Length of the walk: 3½ miles. OS Map Landranger Series 140 Leicester and Coventry (inn GR 253053).

The walk is over land which is now remote but was once a hive of industrial activity with the widespread extraction of coal and minerals. The legacy of this era is the water-filled pits which now attract abundant waterfowl (besides anglers and lovers of quiet places of nature).

Shuttington, a small hilltop village, is an old settlement, as is evidenced by its entry in the Domesday Survey of 1086 and the humble church, which has a fine weatherworn doorway fashioned by Norman masons.

The Walk

Out of the car park turn left on the lane then at once right along a vehicle way which is signed as a footpath. Go through a gate to the

9

St Matthew's church with Norman doorway.

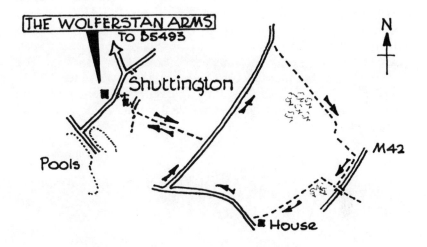

churchyard and admire the Norman arch. Keep to the left of the church (sadly locked) to a gravel path to a cul-de-sac lane. Turn right to walk along a path alongside a garden fence.

Climb a stile to a farm way. Turn left to another stile and a meeting of signed paths. Climb the stile and keep ahead along a fenced way (lovely views now). Climb a stile to a pasture and maintain the direction to a far corner stile by a gate. Walk alongside a left-hand hedge to a stile to a lane.

Turn left for ½ mile. As the lane bends left, climb a stile beside a gate on the right. Walk along a broad cart track.

The way goes beside a wood. Some 400 yards beyond it twists right, then left to regain the old direction. Nearing a motorway the cart track bends sharp right. Keep ahead over the open field towards the motorway. By the fence turn right along a concrete farm road.

Near a bridge is a junction of farm roads. Turn right, then left alongside a wood. The way leads to a lane. Turn right for ⅓ mile. At a junction turn right for 400 yards to a stile you crossed on the outward route. Turn left over the stile and retrace your steps past the church to the pub.

Places of interest nearby

Four miles along lanes to the east is *Twycross Zoo.* Besides the animals in fine surroundings there are restaurants and cafés and picnic areas.

In the valley of the river Anker below Shuttington are *Alvecote Pools.* These are a legacy of subsidence from the coal mines. The pools are now a wonderful nature reserve and a protected Site of Special Scientific Interest. They are a haven for many birds and uncommon insects and, with the rare plants, of great interest to the botanist.

② Bentley
The Horse and Jockey

Some say that this was a coaching inn but the road has always been quite a minor route and the pub is a little isolated and some way outside any town or village. Without the cushion of potential customers living nearby, the Horse and Jockey depends on passing trade and recommendation.

This freehouse is part of the Dugdale estate. The Dugdales are descendants of Warwickshire's famous 16th-century historian Sir William Dugdale; their seat was at the imposing mansion of Merevale Hall a mile or so from Bentley. A more recent Sir William is depicted on the fading sign riding Cloncarrig in the 1952 Grand National.

The Horse and Jockey (up to about four years ago) had been in the care of the Taylor family for almost a century but it was probably a hostelry for some years before this. It has a public bar (where dominoes is enthusiastically played), a lounge, a cosy and snug TV room and a restaurant that has been attractively converted from what was either the barn or the stables. The floor of the public bar is tiled and therefore sympathetic to walkers' boots. This country inn has a

13

modest bill of fare but at modest prices. There is a standard menu in addition to the 'specials of the day', which might include a very tasty home-made curry and giant Yorkshire puddings with a wide range of fillings.

The real ales sold are Bass, Everards Tiger and a guest beer. Four lagers are on offer and the choice of draught cider is between Strongbow and Woodpecker. The garden is bedecked with white furniture for those summer days and the children can play on the grass and swings. A mini-zoo is planned. 'No dogs inside' is the rule at this pub.

The opening hours are 12 noon to 3 pm and 5 pm 'till a flexible closing time' Monday to Friday. On Saturday and Sunday the pub is open all day.

Telephone: 01827 715236.

How to get there: The Horse and Jockey is on the B4116 Birmingham Road 2 miles from Atherstone.

Parking: There is a car park at the side and rear of the pub.

Length of the walk: 2½ miles. OS Map Landranger Series 140 Leicester and Coventry (inn GR 283958).

The walk starts along a broad track through Bentley Park Wood – lovely mixed woodlands here. Past another pub the route follows the Centenary Way. This waymarked route twists a footpath way through Warwickshire and was recently established to mark a century of administration by the County Council.

The Walk

Cross the road from the car park and pass through a gate. The bridleway is signed along a broad forest 'road'. Keep ahead past a cottage and through a gate. Pass a still pool and keep on the main way at junctions. The track leads to a road. Go almost directly over to a lane to regain the old direction.

Within ⅓ mile and opposite Purley Chase Lane take a rather hidden signed path on the right. Climb an old fence stile and walk beside holly bushes to a field. Keep ahead alongside a left-hand hedge and ditch then along the edge of a metal railing fence surrounding a waterworks.

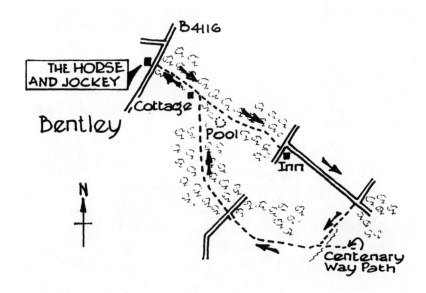

There is a railed barrier to a pasture where horses graze. Keep ahead. Near the far corner the route joins the Centenary Way which emerges over a stile from the left. Cut off the corner of the field right to go over a metal railing barrier.

Maintain the direction at the left-hand side of the field with a wood away to the right. The edge of the field bears right to a vehicle way to a road. Cross the road and turn right for 100 yards. Turn left over a stile beside a gate. Walk along a bold track through the woods. After 400 yards the track divides. Bear right – a lovely snake-like path twists through the trees. When the way again divides after 300 yards take the left-hand fork.

The track leads to a field – arable usually in spite of the pebbly soil. Maintain your direction over the open field aiming 150 yards to the right of a far cottage. Rejoin the outward track and turn left to retrace your steps back to the pub.

Places of interest nearby

Moorwood Rare Breed Working Farm. This is just what its name implies and is 2 miles south-west of Bentley along the lanes. Follow the signs.

Hartshill Hayes Country Park includes remnants of the ancient

Astley Castle ruins.

Forest of Arden. There are many marked nature trails through the woodlands including coppiced woods which provided blocks for the old Atherstone hat manufacturers. The park has an information centre and picnic areas overlooking the valley of the river Trent. To reach the Country Park (about 4 miles south-east of the pub) again follow the many signs.

A few miles further south-east are *Arbury Hall* and *Astley Castle.* The former is said to be the most complete surviving example of 18th-century Gothic Revival in the country. George Eliot was born at South Farm on the estate and she used many of the settings of Arbury in her novels. Overlooking the rather sombre churchyard of Astley church are the ruins of a castle. Built in 1555, the castle was the home of Lady Jane Grey.

③ Barnacle
The Red Lion

The hamlet of Barnacle is probably as far away from the sea as you can get in England – the name is not nautical but derived from the Old English for a slope of barley. This gives us a clue to the history of the Red Lion which for about three centuries has served refreshments for workers on the farms of these arable lands.

This freehouse should not be judged by its rather austere frontage for inside is a simple and homely, genuinely old-fashioned, pub with a warm welcome. The landlord is interested in the footpaths of the area and displays a map of the recent diversions.

This is a pub where darts, dominoes and crib are played with great enthusiasm and where locals meet to discuss the affairs of the parish and the world. There is pride in the Red Lion – brasses gleam and the garden at the rear is carefully tended with plenty of white tables and chairs for those summer days.

There are two bars where the beers served are Brew XI, Bass Bitter and M&B Mild. There is draught Dry Blackthorn cider and a good selection of lagers. The menu for food is not extensive but good standard home-made pub grub – pies, curries, faggots with mushy peas, fish and so on. The prices are modest with the filled jacket potatoes looking especially good value for a hungry walker. The Sunday lunch is a big three-courser and it is recommended that you do the walk first! There is a separate children's menu – burgers, fish fingers, chicken nuggets and all the old 'with chips' favourites.

The opening hours are 11.30 am to 2.30 pm Monday to Friday (to 3 pm Saturday) and 7 pm to 11 pm in the evenings. Sunday hours are 12 noon to 3 pm and 7 pm to 10.30 pm. Sorry, dogs must stay outside.

Telephone: 01203 612100.

How to get there: Barnacle is 6 miles north-east of Coventry. Go along the B4109; 2 miles past the motorway bridge turn right along the lane signed to Barnacle. The Red Lion is at the end of the hamlet on the left.

Parking: There is a small car park at the front of the pub.

Length of the walk: 2½ miles. OS Map Landranger Series 140 Leicester and Coventry area (inn GR 390847).

The walk is over some delightful paths across a wedge of fine countryside which is being squeezed between large conurbations and motorways. These are still mainly arable lands but farmers have co-operated by leaving the pathways unploughed at the borders of the fields. A small addition to the route can be made to visit the Oxford Canal – a contour canal which twists this way and that to avoid further locks during its 77 miles.

The Walk

Out of the car park turn right. Walk along the main street of Barnacle hamlet. Immediately after the road twists sharply to the right turn left down Chapel Lane, signed as a no through road. At the end of the lane turn left to the little Wesleyan chapel which was built in 1844.

Climb a fence stile and keep ahead alongside a right-hand hedge. Go into the next field – again by a right-hand hedge. The path hugs the side of the field, passing a wide hedge gap. At the next hedge gap pass into the following field and continue alongside a right-hand hedge.

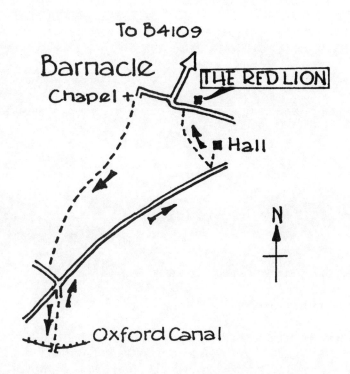

To B4109

Barnacle

Chapel +

THE RED LION

Hall

N

Oxford Canal

Climb a corner fence stile – still there is a hedge on the right-hand side. Follow the border and around bends to the far corner. Maintain the old general heading (right-hand hedges), now heading towards a distant tall electricity pylon.

Climb a corner fence stile and keep ahead. The path borders allotments, then you climb a corner fence stile. Keep ahead along a wide rough track to a road. Turn left to a junction. The route turns left along the lane but to visit the Oxford Canal keep ahead along a vehicle way signed as a no through road and return the same way.

Within about a mile turn left at the drive to Barnacle Hall. Immediately climb a stile to a pasture. Follow the line of a faint tractor way to a stile by a metal gate.

In an arable field follow the right-hand border, then walk alongside a ditch to a hedged track. This leads to the road at Barnacle and the pub is a few steps to the right.

The Oxford Canal.

Places of interest nearby

The *city of Coventry* is 6 miles from Barnacle. It was an old settlement with a Saxon nunnery which in 1043 was converted into a Benedictine priory by Leofric, the Earl of Chester and his wife, the celebrated Countess Godiva. The old cathedral was destroyed in enemy raids during the Second World War – Coventry was the centre of an armaments industry. The new cathedral was designed in an uncompromising modern style by Sir Basil Spence and built alongside the ruins of the burnt-out cathedral church of St Michael.

There are fine shops in the city – many in traffic-free precincts. In one square is an equestrian statue of Lady Godiva.

Coventry Cathedral.

④ Withybrook
The Pheasant

The pub lies alongside the brook of the place-name; many villagers remember the time when it was the Half Moon and was subject to frequent floods. In those days the withies (or willows) were harvested to make baskets and the pub was a simple village hostelry to serve the basketmakers and the farm workers. The locals still talk of the time when old Frank Dexter was the coalman besides serving the ale.

Today this freehouse has been tastefully modernised and extended to create a comfortable country inn where the past is not obliterated. There are old beams, log fires, exposed brickwork on the inner walls and rural memorabilia, including a display of old cycle lamps. There are warm-looking carpets but wisely the stone flags have been retained alongside the bar to accommodate walkers' boots.

There is a very comprehensive menu with additional 'specials of the day' displayed on a blackboard near the door. The price of soup is always a good indication of the price structure – here it was very modest and this is reflected in the rest of the menu. There is a selection of game dishes with venison pie, braised pheasant and roast duck, all popular choices. Fresh fish is always available and the mixture of smoked haddock, sole, haddock, crab, scampi and prawns in the seafood vol-au-vent looked delicious. Vegetarians have a choice from at least six dishes and there are plenty of things to please children.

There are two bars and two 'snug' rooms but with many tables and chairs outside it is particularly pleasant in summertime to be under the rose arbour alongside the bubbling brook.

The real ales served are Courage Directors and John Smith's Bitter. Other draught beers are Webster's Dark Mild, Beamish Stout, Guinness and Kronenbourg 1664. Cider drinkers can enjoy the draught Scrumpy Jack.

Opening hours at the Pheasant on Sundays are 12 noon to 3 pm and 7 pm to 10.30 pm. The rest of the week they are 11 am to 2.30 pm and 6.30 pm to 11 pm.

Telephone: 01455 220480.

Withybrook church.

23

Horses now graze over the 'lost' village of Hopsford.

How to get there: Withybrook is 6 miles south-east of Bedworth along the B4029 and B4112. The pub is on the left at the far end of the village.

Parking: There is a car park at the rear of the pub.

Length of the walk: 3½ miles. OS Map Landranger Series 140 Leicester and Coventry area (inn GR 436840).

Withybrook is in the valley of a fast-flowing tributary of the river Sowe. The walk starts near the little 14th-century church. There is medieval glass in some of the windows and engraved on his altar tomb is a portrait of Christopher Wright (1609) in full armour.

The site of the 'lost' village of Hopsford is passed; here the many ridges, hollows and sunken lines of the streets indicate a fair-sized community.

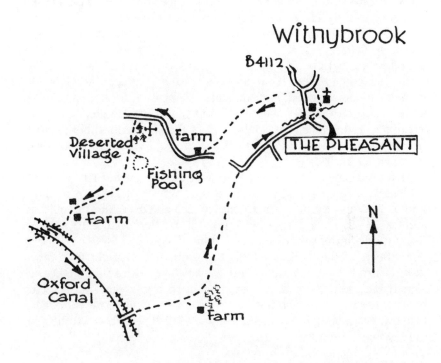

The return leg follows the towpath of the Oxford Canal which was finally completed to connect with the Thames after many delays in 1790. This is also part of the route of the Centenary Way, a long distance path around the county to mark 100 years of local council government.

The Walk

Out of the car park turn left then left again along the vehicle track which borders the brook. Cross the water to the churchyard and continue with the church on the right to a stile to a pasture. Maintain the heading to a stile which will be seen in the distance.

When you reach a lane turn left a few steps to the B4112. Cross to a stile near a seat marked 'Church'. Over the step and fence stiles take the direction indicated by the waymark arrow.

Walk the length of the pasture to a far step stile at the side of a metal gate. Cross the next field to another waymarked stile. Take the

25

arrowed direction to go over the field to pass through a wide hedge gap. Bear slightly left to pass through a row of trees and over a ditch. Veer slightly right to a plank bridge and stile near the corner of the following field.

Follow the right-hand edge of the next pasture for a few yards. Go through a 'squeeze' fence gap and over a stile to a meadow. (Note: It is rather marshy each side of the stile.) Climb to drier land and bear left to a stile to a bridleway. Follow alongside a wooden fence on the left to a gate to a lane. Turn right. Follow the lane around bends. Just before a little pine wood is the site of the old village of Hopsford; now horses graze here.

At the far side of the wood take a bridleway on the left, along a vehicle way. Keep ahead at a junction of ways to pass over a cattle grid. Follow the winding way to pass a farm and go under the railway and canal. At once climb the bank on the left to the tow path. Continue with the water on your left-hand side.

At the next high bridge climb the embankment right to a farm 'road'. Turn left over the canal and railway. Just before a farm take the signed path left (Centenary Way). Through a gate stay by the left-hand wire fence to reach a corner metal gate. Walk along a hedged bridleway to a lane. Keep ahead to the B4112. The pub is a further ¼ mile along the road.

Places of interest nearby

Five miles south-west of Withybrook is *Coombe Countryside Park*. This is in the fine landscaped grounds of *Coombe Abbey*. The Abbey was founded by the Cistercian order in 1150 and by the late 13th century was by far the richest monastic house in the county. Coombe Abbey is now in the hands of the city of Coventry and is a fine place for walks and picnics. The Abbey is part of the history of the land for it was here that James I's young daughter Princess Elizabeth, was staying at the time of the Gunpowder Plot. Lord Harington lived here – he was tutor to the princess.

Church Lawford
The Old Smithy

The building was never in fact a blacksmith's forge – this must have been in the next street which is Smithie Lane. It has been a hostelry for many centuries – at least as far back as the 18th century. A traveller at the turn of the last century called at what was then the Blue Lion Inn and remarked on the sign of the noble beast 'with a most prodigious tail, exactly resembling a mooring line thrown from a ship'. The pub was part of the estate of the Duke of Buccleuch and when it was sold at auction in 1918 it had changed colour and was the White Lion. A decade ago the owners decided there were too many 'Lion' houses and it became the Old Smithy.

Although it obviously relied for trade in past days on locals in the rural community and workers from the fields there was a period when it was run by the People's Public Refreshment Houses Association.

Today's freehouse is a little off the beaten track so has to rely on reputation and recommendation to maintain trade. That it has succeeded is proved by the popularity of the establishment.

There are several rooms and a conservatory and restaurant. The family games room is popular and one finds plenty of non-smoking areas. The decor skilfully incorporates the best of the old with modern comforts. The log fires on those cooler days and the attractive plants in the conservatory are certainly real. Outside one finds a neat beer garden and the play area is loved by the youngsters. Well-behaved dogs too find a welcome at the Old Smithy with its 'flexible' canine policy.

The landlord is very proud of his beers and is the holder of a CAMRA Pub of the Year award. There are six real ales available including Theakston XB and Best, Ansells Mild, Judge's Old Gavel Bender, Ansells Bitter and a 'guest', such as Shipstone's Bitter. Cider drinkers can choose between draught Old English and Dry Blackthorn.

There is a very wide range of dishes listed on the menu; this is divided between headings such as Pasta 'n Pizza, Hot Stuff (spicy things), The Ocean, The Chargrill, Country Fayre and Vegetarian Corner. Children make their selection from Kid's Corner. To add to the difficulty in selecting a meal there are always 'seasonal specials' with items such as Hungarian goulash, Mexican-style lamb shanks and chicken Dijonaise.

The Old Smithy is open all day on Saturday and Sunday. Weekday hours are 11 am to 3 pm and 5.30 pm to 11 pm.

Telephone: 01203 542333.

How to get there: Church Lawford is just off the A428 about midway between Coventry and Rugby. The inn is on the main street in the centre of the village.

Parking: The pub has a large car park at the side.

Length of the walk: 2½ miles. OS Map Landranger Series 140 Leicester and Coventry area (inn GR 450763).

The walk follows the lovely valley of the river Avon. Here in its upper course the water meanders through reeded meadows where the angler has good sport. The route crosses the river by an old mill site. There are rusting mechanisms and traces of the water pools and sluices. On the return leg we pass a farmyard where there is the tower of what was once St Lawrence's church. An old guide book records that almost a century ago the structure was without a roof.

28

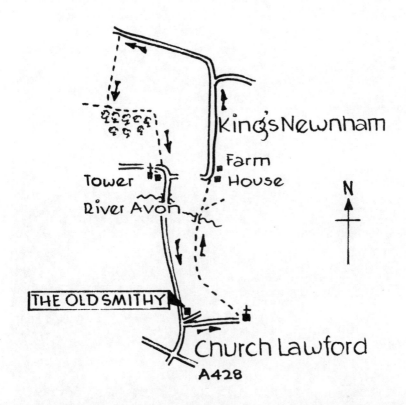

'All honour to the Duke of Buccleuch', exclaimed the writer, for the repairs that were put in hand in 1900.

The Walk

From the car park turn left and cross a lane and the green to Church Road. Turn left to the church. Take the lane signed over the pasture to the left. Walk to the far left-hand corner and climb the stile.

In the next field go a few yards right to another stile and take the signed direction going between newly planted hedges. Pass through a metal gate and keep ahead over a sometimes arable field. Maintain the direction to go over a stile to a pasture, then to a railed footbridge across the river.

Pass the old mill remains and bear right to a double step stile. Two

Coombe Abbey.

paths are indicated. Take the way ahead by the left-hand hedge. Pass through a gate and walk towards the left of a house. Climb a stile and walk to the road.

Keep ahead on the road to climb to a junction. Take the lane ahead. Drop down the hill. Just past a little bridge over a brook go through a metal gate on the left. Walk the length of the pasture and keep ahead to a bold tractor way. Turn left alongside a wood. At the corner turn right to a lane by the farmyard with its church tower.

Turn left, then right along a lane which again crosses the river to return to the Old Smithy.

Places of interest nearby

Four miles to the south of Church Lawford is *Draycote Water*. This is a large reservoir of 240 hectares which supplies Rugby. It is also a country park with noted fishing, providing good sport for the angler catching trout. A sailing club also uses the water and there are pleasant picnic areas. Nearby is the beautiful nature reserve of Draycote Meadows.

6 Earlswood
The Reservoir

The pub is named after the great areas of water nearby – Earlswood Lakes were created in 1810 by building a high dam across the brooks which flowed through two valleys. The water was required then to top up the commercial Stratford-upon-Avon Canal but now this is a great area for recreation. Fishermen line the willow-fringed banks and yachts skim across the water. Bird 'twitchers' look for unusual arrivals – it was the rare Slavonian grebe a year or so back. Above all though, there are many quiet pathways for walking.

The Reservoir is remembered by many for the ballroom that attracted dancers from miles around. Now the dance area has been incorporated in the main old building to create a spacious pub. In those days it was an hotel too but accommodation is no longer available.

This is a pub that really caters for a family clientele. It is a place of fun for youngsters and is the antithesis of the quiet rustic village inn. There are lines of benches and tables, family rooms and outside is a roundabout and the Jungle Bungle. Dogs are not encouraged.

The Jungle Bungle is a large hall crammed full of activity appliances – there are slides and chutes and energy can be expended on climbing ropes and ladders. It would seem to be wise to make a visit here a reward *after* the walk!

The pub is a Miller's Kitchen house and part of the Premier House chain. There is a wide range of food available (including vegetarian dishes) at very modest prices. There is a special menu for junior diners and senior citizens, 'specially chosen for guests with smaller appetites'. There is always a 'specials' board and children love the Miller's Clown and Nelliephant's Treat ice cream. Real ales offered are Davenports and Greenall's Original and a different guest beer is offered each week. For cider drinkers there is draught Strongbow.

The Reservoir is open from 11.30 am all day every day except Sunday, when it opens at 12 noon.

Telephone: 01564 702230.

How to get there: Earlswood is 9 miles south of Birmingham along the B4102. The Reservoir is on the crossroads in the centre of the village.

Parking: There is a large car park at the side of the pub.

Length of the walk: 2 miles. OS Map Landranger Series 139 Birmingham (inn GR 116739).

The route starts with a walk along the ⅓ mile-long dam. From here there is a stunning view along the length of the Lakes. At the end of the dam is the ancient pump house which pushed the water into the canal. (Just along the lane around the corner the delicious Farmer Ted's ice cream is sold.) The path hugs the bank of the reservoir then crosses a causeway to the next lake. The return to the pub is through attractive woodlands.

The Walk

Out of the car park turn left then at once left again at the crossroads. Take the high road to walk along the top of the dam. At the end and immediately before the pump house turn left through a kissing-gate. Follow the waterside path, keeping ahead at junctions. Bear left to continue across the railed metal causeway.

Keep ahead with water each side to a crossroads of tracks. Main-

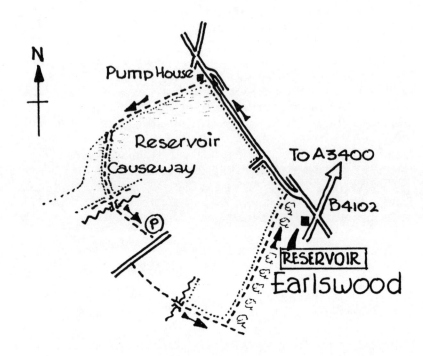

tain the heading over a bridge and through a kissing-gate. Climb the
rise to a car park and a road. Cross the road and turn right for 200
yards. Turn left down a footpath, signed down a vehicle drive.

Within about ⅓ mile cross a bridge (brick parapet). At once go
through a gate left. Regain the old heading with the end of the
reservoir on the left-hand side.

You are now walking along a low earth dam. At the end go over a
wooden bridge and turn left. The path hugs the edge of the reservoir
to a road. Turn right to retrace your steps to the pub.

Places of interest nearby

Earlswood Village Museum is open from March to September in the
village hall. It is run by members of the Earlswood Historical Society. It
contains many interesting village artefacts such as the tools used by the
village blacksmith and wheelwright. There are also photo displays and
features such as the story of when a Heinkel bomber crashed in 1941.

The canal pump house.

Half a mile away is the *Stratford-upon-Avon Canal.* This fascinating waterway was opened in 1816 to carry coal southwards from the Midlands pits and limestone northwards for industry. Now a popular holiday canal, the northern section runs for 12 miles from Kings Norton in Birmingham to Kingswood Junction on the Grand Union Canal.

Midland Bus and Transport Museum, Chapel Lane, Wythall has a fine collection of vintage buses and commercial vehicles. The museum is open every weekend from 9 am to 7 pm throughout the year. Wythall is 3 miles west of Earlswood and the museum is near the church.

⑦ Lapworth
The Boot Inn

With this pub backing onto the Stratford-upon-Avon Canal one might think that trade in past days came from the commercial barge traffic. However, the address gives the real clue. The Boot is on the Old Warwick Road; this was the main highway from Birmingham to the county town and it was a coaching inn. There are plenty of buildings at the back where horses were stabled.

At the time of writing there had recently been a change of management and a major refurbishment was about to take place. At the moment the 400-year old Whitbread house presents an old world ambience with inglenooks, oak furniture and prints of the countryside of yesteryear, and one assumes this style will remain although updated to modern standards. I was assured too that the blazing log fire will continue to give a warm welcome in wintertime.

There is a bar, a lounge and private dining room. Four ales are always available – Flowers Best, Tetley, Boddingtons and Old

Speckled Hen. Strongbow cider is on draught and the Boot specialises in New World wines (probably recommended by the Australian chef).

The aim in the future is to offer dishes from many parts of the world besides more simple pub fare. A popular vegetarian choice could be the Piedmont red peppers with salad and crusty bread. From the large choice of fowl and fish items the Cromer crab with salad and lemon mayonnaise looked tempting. Children's portions of the dishes are available. The Boot is open all day Saturday and Sunday; the weekday hours are 11 am to 3 pm and 5.30 pm to 11 pm. The welcome to well-behaved dogs is indicated by the bowl of water by the door although Fido may prefer to stay with his master outside in the garden by the tables and benches.

Telephone: 01564 782464.

How to get there: The Boot is on the left of the B4439 2 miles south-east of Hockley Heath.

Parking: There is a large car park at the side of the pub.

Length of the walk: 2½ miles. OS Map Landranger Series 139 Birmingham (inn GR 182712).

The walk begins along the towpath of the Stratford-upon-Avon Canal, which here climbs by the Lapworth flight of locks from the Avon valley up to the Birmingham plateau. Through parkland there is an attractive view of the rear of the National Trust's Packwood House. (A short diversion can be made from the route to visit the 16th-century house with its famous topiary.) The return leg starts at Lapworth church which has a beautiful spire and unusual 15th-century chantry chapel.

The Walk

Go along the track at the right-hand corner of the car park to the canal. Cross the water and turn left along the towing path. You will be walking at the side of the Lapworth flight of locks.

By the lock-keeper's cottage leave the waterway to go along a rough vehicle way through a farmyard. Follow the track to a lane. Turn right for ¼ mile to a road junction. If you want to visit Packwood House keep ahead. Otherwise turn left up steps and along

37

a signed footpath.

Stay at the side of a lawn, then to the right of a house. Keep ahead over stiles to a large field which is often under the plough. Follow along the right-hand boundary to a stile to parkland where sheep graze. Regain the old direction, never far from the left-hand border. The path is to the right of a house, to a stile beside a gate onto a lane. Turn left to a crossroads. Go straight over. The lane goes by a pond where ducks glide, then to Lapworth church. Just before the church and by the war memorial turn left down Tapster Lane.

Within 200 yards the next path is over a stile on the left. Walk near the left-hand border of the field to a stile to the end of a large garden. Follow the arrowed direction to continue to the left of a pond to another stile. Cut over the pasture to a further stile. Waymarks and more stiles show the route through fields and a cricket ground.

Maintain the heading through a long meadow to a stile by a gate onto the B4439. At once turn left down the track to the towing path. Turn right to go under the road bridge. Keep by the canal to walk by a lock. Rejoin the outer route by the cottage and retrace your steps by the flight of locks and over the water to the pub.

Places of interest nearby

Packwood House is open from April to the end of September, from Wednesday to Sunday. It is a fascinating timber-framed Tudor house containing a wealth of fine tapestries and furniture. On the old stables are some magnificent sundials, and the lovely gardens are noted for the yew topiary depicting the Sermon on the Mount.

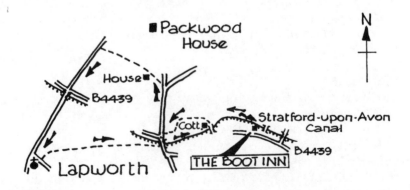

Packwood House.

Two miles east of the Boot is *Baddesley Clinton Hall,* another National Trust property. It is a moated manor house from the 14th century. The beauty of this place is that it has been little changed since 1634 and children love to discover the cleverly concealed priest holes. There are portraits of the Ferrers family and a little chapel. Along a shady pathway is St Michael's church where the churchyard is a carpet of bluebells in springtime. The tower was built about 1500 by Nicholas Brome in remorse for having killed a priest. Baddesley Clinton Hall is open Wednesday to Sunday from March until the end of October.

Kenilworth
8
The Clarendon Arms

This pub is cheek by jowl with another hostelry but there is quite a contrast. The other is large and pleasant but part of a nationwide group – the Clarendon Arms is a humble inn but with a wealth of nice features. There are wattle and daub walls upstairs so the age of the building must go back some hundreds of years.

The pub is named after the Clarendon family. Charles II gave the castle (by this time in ruins) to the Hyde family of his chief minister Lord Clarendon. It remained with this family until 1937.

Some people suggested the Clarendon Arms may once have been

an abattoir but this was soon discounted by locals who remember it as a real, basic pub for the labourers of Castle Green with just a simple small bar and a serving hatch for the off sales. Since those far off days, bars in the narrow building (a Tennent's managed house) have been extended to the rear to provide quite deceptively spacious accommodation. There are several lounges and snugs and some of the rooms have been designated as 'non-smokers'. Some tables are bookable.

There are always 'specials of the day' displayed on a blackboard but the standard menu offers a good choice with the burgers modestly described as 'probably the best in Warwickshire'!

The Desperate Dan Pie – a huge concoction of beef, mushrooms, vegetables and potatoes sounds just right for a ravenous walker and there is a Hungry Hippo menu for the youngsters. Specials might include jacket potato wedges with a garlic dip and Jamaican-style chicken (chicken in a hot spicy sauce). There are always 'Naughty Puds' available. You may be tempted by the Drunken Druid's Delight – a delicious mixture of biscuit, rum mousse and white chocolate.

The choice of real ales is excellent – Courage Directors and Best, John Smith's, Ansells Mild, Morland Old Speckled Hen, with Brew XI as a 'guest'. Cider is a choice between Scrumpy Jack and Wood-pecker. 'No dogs' is the rule in the Clarendon Arms and there is a small patio outside with a few tables and benches.

The opening hours are Monday to Saturday 11 am to 3 pm and 5.30 pm to 11 pm with all day opening on Sunday.

Telephone: 01926 52017.

How to get there: The Clarendon Arms is just off the B4103 at Castle Green, Kenilworth, outside the castle walls.

Parking: There is no parking at this pub. There is a public car park (no charge) outside the castle walls which is only a few yards from the Clarendon Arms.

Length of the walk: 3 miles. OS Map Landranger Series 140 Leicester and Coventry area (inn GR 2800723).

The first few steps of the walk are alongside the massive castle walls. We then cross Finham brook which was dammed to create a huge defensive lake for the castle. The water stretched as far as The

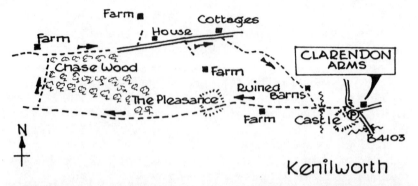

Kenilworth

Pleasance – created by Henry V as a retreat, perhaps for some dalliance and romance! The route is over the hollows and mounds, all that remains to remind us of past splendour. A path by Chase Wood follows – it is named after a famous steeplechase. Over the distant trees a great hilltop mansion and church can just be seen. The house is Honiley Hall from the late 17th century. The church with a fine spire was perhaps designed by Sir Christopher Wren who lived a mile or so distant for the last few years of his life. The return leg over the meadows gives magnificent vistas of the sandstone castle.

The Walk

From the car park walk alongside the castle walls with the castle on the left-hand side. Go through a squeeze stile to a meadow. Bear right by a thatched cottage to pass through another squeeze stile to a vehicle way. Turn left to cross Finham brook. Keep ahead to pass by a farm. The vehicle way becomes a footpath and a stile leads to the site of The Pleasance.

Walk over the rough land to a far corner stile. Continue by a left-hand, then a right-hand hedge. Maintain the same heading to 'nudge' Chase Wood, then walk alongside a row of trees. The path stays at the edge of fields to a signed junction of tracks. Turn right.

Climb the rise, soon walking at the side of a right-hand wood to a farm drive. Turn right. The drive becomes a lane. After almost a mile and opposite red brick cottages, take a signed path over a stile on the right. Take the direction indicated. The route over the fields is marked by stiles and waymark arrows.

Go by some ruined brick barns and continue to a stile onto the original outward vehicle track. Turn left and retrace your steps back to the car park.

Kenilworth Castle.

Places of interest nearby

A visit to *Kenilworth Castle* is a must. The great fortification was started in 1122 when Henry I gave the rocky outcrop to his Treasurer, Geoffrey de Clinton. Henry II thought it too opulent for a commoner and took over the castle. There were many additions over the next 400 years. After the Civil War in 1649 Parliament ordered Colonel Hawksworth to 'slight' (partially destroy) the fortification. The castle was presented to the nation in 1937 by Sir John Siddeley and, administered by English Heritage, is now open every day.

Half a mile east of the pub (in *Abbey Park*) are the ruins of a great Augustinian priory which was also founded in 1122 by Geoffrey de Clinton (see above). It became an abbey about the middle of the 15th century and it is believed de Clinton is buried here.

Weston under Wetherley
The Bull Inn

The 'under Wetherley' part of the place-name comes from the Old English for 'under a hunting wood' and there are still fine woods not far distant. The Bull Inn is about three centuries old and was originally a cottage, becoming a pub around 1890 when it was converted to serve the farm workers. In more recent years an extension has been sympathetically added.

It is still rather remote and well away from the centre of the village so depends greatly for trade on passing traffic and recommendation. It certainly has a fine reputation (with booking advised for larger than average parties) for its varied menu and especially the home-cooked 'specials of the day'. There are at least four from which to make a difficult choice; one of these is usually a roast. Vegetarians always have a good selection from which to choose and the spicy broccoli au gratin is popular. Families are especially welcome to the Sunday lunch when children's portions are available.

The real ales on offer in this Marston's house are their Bitter and Pedigree beers with a good selection of draught lagers and cider. The daily opening hours are 12 noon to 3 pm and 6.30 pm to 11 pm but note that food is not served on Sunday evenings.

The bar (where darts is played) and the restaurant have a warm homely appearance with 'chunky' tables and saddleback chairs. There are old prints on the walls and interesting old posters – how about sending a halfpenny postcard for a price list of game foods or some puttees (without spats) for 5s 6d?

Outside one can sit on benches beneath the silver birches – which is where your dog should remain on guard.

Telephone: 01926 632392.

How to get there: The Bull Inn is 5 miles north-east of Royal Leamington Spa along the B4453. The pub is at the far end of Weston under Wetherley.

Parking: You can park at each side of the pub.

Length of the walk: 3 miles. OS Map Landranger Series 151 Stratford-upon-Avon (inn GR 368694).

The walk is through the rich farmlands of the valley of the river Leam (a tributary of the Avon). The early path crosses the site of a great earthwork settlement but ploughing still goes on over this historic area. The route passes the 13th-century red sandstone church of St John the Baptist – there is a giant Celtic cross in the churchyard. There is an old bridge across the reeded river Leam which has withstood the waters for many centuries. Another old place of worship overlooks the meadows at Hunningham.

In the church there is the work of Norman masons. The return leg is alongside the river, then along a lane which crosses the water over a medieval bridge.

The Walk

Out of the car park turn right and walk a few steps along the B4453. When the road turns sharp right keep ahead along the lane signed to Hunningham. Within 200 yards your path is signed over a stile on the left. Walk alongside a left-hand hedge.

Climb a corner stile then maintain the direction to go over a footbridge. Again keep the heading over another stile and follow the arrowed way at the side of the field. Turn the corner to the next

45

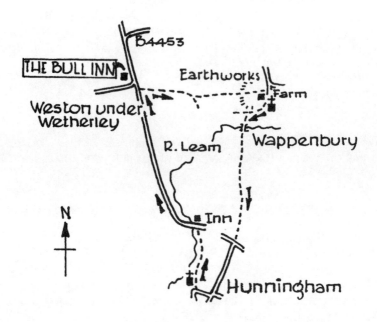

corner, and go through the hedge gap.

Two paths are signed here (although the post was wobbly and may soon disappear!). Turn left and strike out over the open field, aiming well to the left of the church tower and large barns.

Go over a bridge in the opposite boundary and climb steps to the next field. Still to the left of the barns, go over another open field (the site of the ancient settlement) to a hedge gap onto a lane at Wappenbury. Turn right then keep ahead at a junction of ways to proceed to the right of the church. By a lamppost and railing gate turn right.

Walk along a vehicle way. At the end turn left through a hunting gate. Keep ahead to cross the river Leam, then go over a sheep pasture to pass through another hunting gate. Walk at the side of two fields to a gate onto a road. Cross to the opposite lane (signed Offchurch).

The medieval bridge at Hunningham.

Within ⅓ mile and just past a farm turn right down a lane signed Hunningham church. As the lane turns sharp left, keep ahead to the gate to the churchyard. Do not pass through but bear right alongside the fence to a stile into a pasture. Follow the left-hand fence, then in the open pasture bear left to climb a stile in the far left-hand corner.

Follow the riverbank for 150 yards then climb a stile to a meadow on the right. Walk alongside a left-hand fence for 100 yards then climb another stile back to the riverside path. Follow this to the right to a lane. Turn left to cross the medieval bridge. The lane leads back to the B4453 and the pub.

Places of interest nearby

A guide book to *Royal Leamington Spa* (5 miles from the Bull Inn) says that it is one of the finest towns in England for the 'calm dignity of its streets, the beauty of its gardens and the unspoiled loveliness of the little river'. The first spa bath was built about two centuries ago but the healing waters were known in the days of the first Elizabeth. There are many elegant buildings and fine shops and Jephson Gardens (laid out in 1834) are a delight.

10 Leek Wootton
The Anchor

It is always a pity when the history of a pub is obscure and unrecorded. The name of the Anchor is also intriguing – surely there is a story to tell here when the village could hardly be further from the sea! What we find in this M&B house is a high standard of comfort and meals. It is particularly welcoming during wintertime when the open fires are burning. The polished brass gleams and there is a particularly extensive range of horse brasses.

The choice of real ales is between Bass, Brew XI and a guest brew, such as Old Speckled Hen. There is Dry Blackthorn draught cider and a good range of wines. The menu includes good standard fare but there are a few unusual dishes including Anchor Pie (which sounds as if it should be fish but is actually chicken coated with barbecue sauce and topped with ham and cheese). The salmon and dill pie is popular and there are always dishes for vegetarians. There is a Gold 25 Card for the 55+ age group which gives 25% off the price of meals.

For children there is a special Hippo Menu. This contains all the old chip-accompanied favourites including chicken nuggets, fish bites, sausages and beefburgers. For the health-conscious we find an assortment of salads but perhaps they will also fall for the traditional 'puds' like jam roly-poly or spotted dick.

Dogs are not allowed in the bars; there is a garden with benches and tables. Opening hours are 11 am to 3 pm and 6 pm to 11 pm (Monday to Saturday) and normal hours on Sunday.

Telephone: 01926 53355.

How to get there: Leek Wootton is about 3 miles north of Warwick along the A429 and across the A46. The Anchor is at a road junction in the centre of the village.

Parking: There is a large car park behind the pub.

Length of the walk: 2 miles. OS Map Landranger Series 151 Stratford-upon-Avon (inn GR 289690).

Leek Wootton is on a lofty site above the valley of the river Avon so there are pleasant views. It is an old village recorded in the Domesday Book of 1086. There are timber-framed buildings capped by thatch but new developments have been well assimilated. The route of the walk is mainly around a fairly recently constructed golf course but the old pathways have been treated sympathetically and diverted. The former great mansion of Woodcote, 1861, is passed; the building is now a police headquarters.

The Walk

Turn left from the car park then immediately left again along Woodcote Lane. Within 300 yards turn left along a path signed up steps. Keep ahead along a hedged way. At a junction of tracks by a thatched cottage turn right, then climb a stile to a field. Keep ahead alongside a hedge and continue to a stile to the golf course.

Turn right and follow the boundary around corners to pass near Woodcote. Keep along the path to reach woods and follow the waymarked route, passing (not climbing) a fence stile. Go over a low plank bridge and through trees to a signed junction of ways.

Turn left through bushes and trees and stay in the woods, crossing a wide bridge. Climb a triple stile out of the woods. Bear left over a path across meadows. Within 200 yards climb a stile on the left back

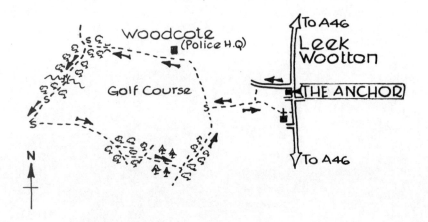

into the golf course. Follow the path marked by green and yellow posts. Take care after about 300 yards to swing right to walk along a concrete pathway, passing tee number 8.

The path soon enters woods along a way signed to '4th tee North' and still marked with green and yellow posts. At the next sign '4th tee North' keep ahead to keep this sign on the left. Within 30 yards bear left off the concrete way along a path through the trees.

Cross other tracks to a golf fairway. Cross over to a fir wood. Maintain the heading along a straight path through the trees.

At a bold wide track bear left along the track, then right along a path just before the golf course. Follow the path out of the wood and keep ahead over the golf course. There is a fine view now far over Warwick with the tower of St Mary's church prominent. Where directed turn left to the stile you climbed earlier. Turn right over this stile and retrace your steps at the side of the field and over the stile to the junction of ways by the thatched cottage.

Keep ahead (with the cottage on the left). The hedged way leads to the drive by the church. Turn left to the road. The Anchor is 400 yards to the left.

Places of interest nearby

Warwick has a lot to offer. Besides the great castle (open every day), St Mary's church has much of interest and a tower which rises 174 ft above the town. Of the collegiate church which was built in 1123 only

A lock on the Hatton flight.

the crypt survives today; much was consumed in a great fire in 1694. However, the Beauchamp Chapel built between 1443 and 1464 is said to be the finest chantry (endowed) chapel in the land.

Three miles to the south of Leek Wootton by the junction of the A46 with the Solihull road is the *Grand Union Canal.* There is a very informative notice and a picnic site by a lock. The famous Hatton flight of 21 locks starts here where the waterway climbs to the Birmingham plateau at 337 ft above sea level.

⑪ Hatton
The Waterman

The Waterman overlooks the spectacular Hatton flight of locks on the Grand Union Canal. It is sited on a little hill some hundred yards from the actual waterway, which may throw doubt on it being a 'canal' pub used by bargees in past days. That said, it has obviously been closely connected with the canal as is evidenced by the interesting array of old photographs in the lounge. Of especial note are those taken at the opening by the Duke of York in 1934 of the widened locks to take larger craft. This was a well-intentioned but unsuccessful attempt to compete with the railways. Another of the old prints depicts the pub about a hundred years ago; the 16th-century building (then called the New Inn) was at that time very small and a pony and trap is shown outside.

Today the inn has been sympathetically extended and modernised to provide a very pleasant ambience, including a timber-framed room where smoking is not allowed. There is also a public bar and lounge bar.

The Waterman has won awards for its 'pub grub'; the menu is not extensive but offers excellent value for money, including home-made soup and a giant 'steakwich', and the Waterman's mixed grill is very popular. There is always a vegetarian dish of the day and a separate children's menu and excellent salad bar. Dogs are not excluded from the public bar but should not venture into the other parts of the pub. The beers available in this Greenall's tenanted pub include Davenports, Tetley and Bass and the trio of draught cider is Strongbow, Woodpecker and Scrumpy Jack.

There is a terrace with fine views across to the canal and a huge outdoor area with a multitude of play equipment. Youngsters will appreciate the grass on which to chase and play. The pub is open all day (Monday to Saturday) with normal Sunday hours.

Telephone: 01926 492427.

How to get there: The Waterman is about 2½ miles west of Warwick, on the left-hand side of the A4177 when coming from that direction.

Parking: There is a car park at the side of the pub.

Length of the walk: 1½ miles. OS Map Landranger Series 151 Stratford-upon-Avon (inn GR 243671).

The outward leg of the walk is over gentle countryside to a far farmstead. The return is alongside some of the locks of the Hatton flight on the Grand Union Canal. There are 21 locks on the flight over a distance of 2 miles. They lift the craft 146 ft and each one holds 50,000 gallons of water. The former narrow locks are alongside and are now used as overflow weirs; the grooves worn by the towing ropes on the brickwork can be seen.

The Walk

Go to the rear of the pub to the field. Cross diagonally towards a white house and climb the corner stile. Continue to the canal and cross the bridge. Keep ahead along a signed path through fields to cross a railway.

Maintain the direction over the open arable field to pass through a far wide hedge gap. Bear slightly left again over an open field aiming to the chimneys of a farmhouse on a distant hill. Go over the foot-bridge across a brook.

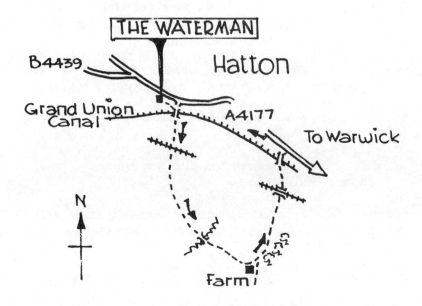

Keep the heading, now climbing a hill. Go over a double step stile which adjoins a metal gate. Follow the arrowed direction along the head of a pasture with the farm now on your right-hand side. Pass through a corner gate and at once turn left alongside a wire fence, then through a wide hedge gap.

Maintain the heading for about 150 yards alongside the wood, then bear left over the open field making for the tunnel under the railway. Beyond the tunnel is a winding path through scrubland. Keep ahead through a metal gate to the canal. Gain the towing path and walk alongside the waterway to rejoin the outward route back to the Waterman.

Places of interest nearby

A mile from the Waterman is the *Hatton Craft Centre*. Besides the wide array of skilled craftsmen there are animals to see and nature walks. The centre is open daily.

In *Warwick* there are museums and the major attractions of the castle and St Mary's church. The castle (open daily) dates from the

The Grand Union Canal.

first defensive works erected by Ethelfleda, daughter of Alfred the Great, in AD 916. This was followed by the Norman motte and bailey castle. The visit to the castle warrants a lengthy period as there is so much of interest, including realistic wax model displays and outside entertainments.

St Mary's church mostly dates from the rebuilding after the great fire of 1694 although the crypt of the collegiate building of 1123 survived the flames. The richly decorated Beauchamp Chapel, built in accordance with the will of Richard Beauchamp, Earl of Warwick, who died in 1439, is said to be the finest chantry chapel in the country.

Claverdon
12 The Red Lion

In its publicity the pub rightly stresses two aspects: its hilltop situation which gives beautiful views far over the Warwickshire countryside, and the cuisine – home cooked meals with a country flavour.

The place bears a popular inn name but this Red Lion has a unique history and appearance. To give you some idea of the original building you can see a photograph dated 1921 in the bar – it was in those days little more than a tiny timber-framed bungalow. This was a private house and a few hundred years old; it formed the core of the present pub. Before the 1930s the Red Lion was near the church but the ancient bungalow was sympathetically extended when the licence was transferred.

There are plenty of the old beams of the original building in the large lounge, which has a welcoming feel – in spite of the tales recounted by the landlord of a rather obscure ghost. The lounge has that magnificent view but the bar is more basic and has the dartboard and pool table.

The old forge, Claverdon.

There is a menu but take care to study the specials board, which lists more unusual dishes such as beef and beer crumble or pork and mushroom fricassee. The choice of beers is excellent, including Flowers Best Bitter (this is a Whitbread house), Morland Old Speckled Hen, Boddingtons Bitter and a guest beer such as Castle Eden's Green Bullet. There is draught Strongbow for the cider drinker.

There is a pleasant garden (of course with that view) with plenty of benches and tables. Alongside is an excellent children's playground with the sort of fun equipment which makes an oldie wish to be young again. Dogs, I'm afraid, are not welcome inside the pub.

The opening hours are 12 noon to 3 pm and 6 pm to 11 pm (Monday to Saturday). The only variation on Sunday is the normal 7 pm to 10.30 pm in the evenings. Meal hours are a little flexible but usually slightly shorter than the drinking times.

Telephone: 01926 842291.

How to get there: Claverdon is on the A4189 Warwick to Henley road 5 miles west of Warwick. The Red Lion is on the edge of the village on the left coming from Warwick.

57

Claverdon

Parking: There is a large car park at the side of the pub.

Length of the walk: 2½ miles. OS Map Landranger Series 151 Stratford-upon-Avon (inn GR 201647).

Claverdon was mentioned in the Domesday Survey of 1086 as 'Claefer Dun' or Clover Down – and it is said there is still plenty of clover to be seen. The walk certainly starts off through pastoral farmland after passing the old forge. This building dates from the 17th century and has a strange wooden horseshoe-shaped entrance. In the church (much altered by the Victorians) is a monument to Thomas Spencer who was a distant relative of the Princess of Wales (who was Lady Diana Spencer before her marriage).

The Walk

Coming out of the car park turn left along the A4189. Within a few steps turn left down Church Road by the former blacksmith's forge. After about 400 yards turn left down the drive of Park Farm. Within a step or two go through a gate and at once climb a ladder stile to the pasture on the left.

Drop down the hill to a fence stile (difficult for dogs!). Continue at the side of an often cultivated field (hedge on the left). Go through a far corner hedge gap and keep ahead for 75 yards then bear left along a wide cart track to the road.

Turn left then immediately right down a lane signed to Lye Green. Immediately there is a stile to climb by a gate on the right. In the meadow follow the arrowed direction near the left-hand border to a rough fence stile and step stile.

Regain the old heading alongside the left-hand boundary to another corner stile alongside a metal gate. Keep the old direction straight across the field to another metal gate. Do not go through but turn left, still at the side of the field, to climb a step stile.

Follow the arrowed heading up the field to a gate by a water trough. Go along the arrowed route but beware of nettles. The path leads to a stile and meeting of paths by some barns. Take the left-hand way to pass by the stables and with the barns immediately on your left, to reach a stile to a lane. Turn left.

At once take a signed path on the right over a stile. Over a foot-bridge enter a field. Keep by the right-hand border. Climb a corner stile. Keep ahead to go over a stile and footbridge. Swing right to walk to the right of a house. Join the drive which becomes a lane leading to a road.

Turn left. Follow the road for a little over ½ mile. At the far side of the green of Lye Green is a crossroads. Turn left along a lovely narrow lane. Within ⅓ mile take a signed path over a stile right. Cross the pasture to another stile to an often arable field. Walk by the left-hand border. After about 400 yards and just past a large tree turn left through a wide hedge gap.

Cut across the open field to a gate to the right of a white house. On the road turn left back to the Red Lion.

Places of interest nearby

Warwick is 5 miles away along the A4189. The great castle dates from a defensive fortification erected at the time of Ethelfleda in about AD

916. The Normans appreciated the site above the river Avon and built a castle here but most of the present buildings were constructed by the Beauchamp family from the mid 14th century. The castle is open daily and includes waxworks and displays showing the lives of past inhabitants; there are family and concessionary entrance tickets.

Towering over Warwick is the 174 ft high tower of St Mary's church. This is the 'new' tower as much of the old building was destroyed in the great fire of 1694. Some parts survived including the Norman crypt, the chancel and the 15th-century Beauchamp Chapel. There are fine brasses which also pre-date the fire.

A walk around Warwick discloses some fascinating buildings, including two gateways and the ancient timber-framed Lord Leycester's Hospital.

Wootton Wawen
The Navigation Inn

The pub nudges the Stratford-upon-Avon Canal; in days long past it was a commercial inn so dates from the start of the waterway. It was in 1793 that the authorising Act of Parliament was passed and the whole length was finally opened in 1816. The primary trade was to convey coal southwards from the Midland mines and limestone and grain in the other direction.

Thirty or so years ago the cut was derelict and overgrown, but it was rescued by the National Trust to be reopened for holiday craft in 1964. It is now in the care of British Waterways.

Whereas the navvies constructing the canal and bargees on the horse-towed craft used to frequent the Navigation Inn (as is pictured on the sign) it is now popular with the 'captains' and crews of pleasure boats. The customers also include fishermen and walkers who enjoy the ambience of the flower-bedecked pub. There are mock beams but the warmth of the welcome is genuine; the place has recently been refurbished with red carpeting so take care if boots are muddy. There is one large bar (with a family section) where dogs are welcome and a restaurant where they are excluded.

The real ales in this Whitbread pub are Flowers Pedigree, Everards Tiger and Boddingtons Bitter. There is also usually a guest beer and Strongbow and Woodpecker available on draught.

There is a fairly modest menu of good standard pub fare and always a choice for children and those who prefer a vegetarian dish. When I called there were Balti specials on offer; basket meals are a speciality too and the Sunday lunch is very popular.

Outside is a splendid garden with benches and tables and plenty of grass where children can chase and play. They can also clamber up into the tree house. There is shade for those hot summer days where you can watch the boats drifting by on the canal alongside.

The pub is open all day (11 am to 11 pm) during the summer months (and on Saturday in winter). The Monday to Friday hours in the winter and the Sunday hours in the summer are standard.

Telephone: 01564 792676.

How to get there: Wootton Wawen is on the A3400 about 6 miles north-west of Stratford. The Navigation Inn is on the right immediately before the village coming from Stratford.

The canal basin.

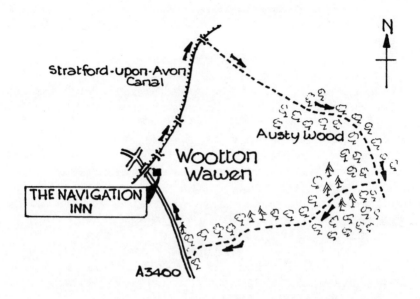

Parking: There is a car park beside the pub.

Length of the walk: 2½ miles. OS Map Landranger Series 151 Stratford-upon-Avon (inn GR 160629).

The walk starts along the towing path beside the Stratford Canal and the next stage is through the delightful Austy Woods. These are mixed woodlands – coniferous and deciduous trees with plenty of undergrowth to attract wildlife. Later the route is beside a field from where there are wide views across to the Cotswolds.

The Walk

From the car park cross the main road and turn right. Follow the winding path under the magnificent aqueduct. At once climb the path left to the towing path. Turn left over the road. Follow the towing path for about ½ mile. At the bridge numbered 51 go over the canal. (Note the split down the middle of the bridge which meant the towing horses did not need to be unhitched.)

Walking away from the canal follow the wide path between hedges.

63

The track gradually climbs to enter woods. Keep ahead. On the summit and immediately before a gate to a field turn right along a tractor way. The track emerges from the trees to a large field. Keep along the border to the very far end. Turn the corner left.

Within a hundred yards turn right along a path through a wood to the road. Cross over and turn right. The Navigation Inn is about ½ mile away on the right.

Places of interest nearby
The village of Wootton Wawen is said to be the oldest in Warwickshire. There is much Saxon work in the lovely church – half the tower is from this period. Near the church is *Wootton Hall.* The great house was built in an Italianate style in 1637 and it is said the ghost of the Grey Lady (Mrs Fitzherbert – the wife of King George IV) is seen.

Four miles south is the village of Wilmcote and *Mary Arden's House.* This was the 16th-century childhood home of William Shakespeare's mother and is open to the public daily. In the grounds is a fine collection of agricultural implements.

14 Flecknoe
The Old Olive Bush

This seems a strange name for a pub in the lonely Warwickshire countryside far from the Mediterranean. Two hundred or so years ago the house opposite was the pub but at the turn of the 19th century the present building was extensively damaged in a fire. Today this is a very convivial hostelry, which is the centre of village life with the old post office long gone. The cricketers gather here and darts and quizzes are very popular.

The owner of this freehouse (a Cordon Bleu chef) spent 14 years in Italy and it is no surprise therefore that there are plenty of Italian dishes on offer together with recipes that originate in Turkey and the former Persia. Families are made very welcome at the Old Olive Bush but the children would probably prefer the old favourites available with chips.

The choice of real ales rests between Bass Bitter and Websters. For lager drinkers there is Pilsner, and there is cider on draught. The pub has a homely bar and a lounge with French windows onto the car

The replica stocks at Flecknoe.

park and the very pretty garden which is brimming with flowers. Darts are played in the separate games room.

The hours of this pub are somewhat flexible but are generally 12 noon to 2.30 pm, and 7 pm to 11 pm (10.30 pm Sunday). There is a notice 'Never mind the dog – beware of the owner' and this gives a clue that well-behaved canine friends can find a welcome here.

Telephone: 01788 891134.

How to get there: Flecknoe is 4 miles west of Daventry. Turn north off the A425 and follow the lanes to the hamlet. The pub is in the centre of Flecknoe.

Parking: There is a car park at the rear of the pub.

Length of the walk: 3½ miles. OS Map Landranger Series 151 Stratford-upon-Avon (inn GR 517635).

These are rich agricultural lands with mixed farming. On the walk the Grand Union Canal (which twists its way towards

Daventry and London) is crossed. The waterway consists of many former independent canals which were amalgamated in 1929. There are 166 locks to negotiate on the full route! Almost opposite the pub is a replica of the ancient stocks.

The Walk

Out of the car park turn right to pass in front of the pub. Keep ahead at a road junction and stay on the main road at a second junction. There is an old school building; immediately turn right along Bush Hill Lane. Within 200 yards the road bends left. Keep ahead for a step or two. By a small Dutch barn turn 90 degrees right along a signed path. Walk at the side of the lawn with the houses on the right.

Follow the path to a lane. Turn left. At the end of the lane go through a gate into a field. Follow the arrowed direction of a bridleway to a hedge gap near the far left-hand corner of the field. Cross a ditch to go into the next field. Follow a left-hand hedge.

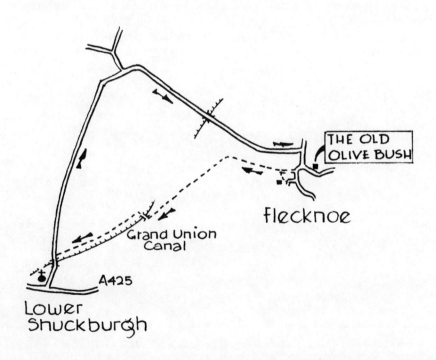

THE OLD OLIVE BUSH

flecknoe

Grand Union Canal

A425

Lower Shuckburgh

Halfway along go through a hedge gap left and follow a track across the (often arable) open field.

Go through another hedge gap. In the field maintain the old direction and similarly in the following field continue on to cross a canal bridge. At once turn left. (There is a fence here to the canal towing path for a shortened walk although there is unfortunately no official link between the towing path and the bridleway.)

The bridleway hugs the waterway to a lane at Lower Shuckburgh. Turn right and keep ahead at a junction. The lane goes over the Grand Union Canal. Continue to a T-junction. Turn right to Flecknoe. At the next T-junction the Old Olive Bush is to the left.

Places of interest nearby

Four miles to the west of Flecknoe is Napton on the Hill. Even higher on the hill above the village is a magnificent *windmill*. It has been lovingly restored in recent years.

Draycote Water Country Park is based on the man-made lake. There are plenty of picnic facilities and for naturalists the lake is a great mecca for many species of waterfowl. A sailing club uses the water for sport. The park is reached along lanes and the A426 5 miles north-west of Flecknoe.

⑮ Wellesbourne
The Stag's Head

Today there is just one Wellesbourne but in past days there were two – Wellesbourne Hastings and Wellesbourne Mountford, both named after noted local families. Wellesbourne Mountford was on the southern fringes of the modern village with magnificent old buildings clustered around Chestnut Green.

Among these old buildings is the Stag's Head which is capped by thatch. Old prints in the bars show that it has been splendidly restored and differs little from the hostelry of a century ago. It was originally two cottages which were knocked into one to form the Stag's Head.

In those far off days it would appear to have been a popular place for agricultural workers. They became a campaigning lot and when the pub was too small for their numbers they gathered for meetings on the green. In 1872, led by Joseph Arch, they formed themselves into a trade union for agricultural workers; the event is commemorated by an annual parade and marked by a plaque under a tree.

The restoration of the Whitbread pub has been approved by English Heritage and the quality and range of beers has ensured its entry in the CAMRA guide. The real ales available include Spitfire, 6X, Landlord Bitter, Boddingtons, and Marston's Pedigree. Strongbow cider is also available on draught.

The hours of opening are 11.30 am to 2.30 pm and 6 pm to 11 pm Monday to Saturday and 12 noon to 3 pm and 7 pm to 10.30 pm on Sundays. The food offered is good standard pub fare from a menu but the landlord is always willing to prepare anything special on request. There are some unusual meals listed including, for example, mixed vegetable dimsum – a Chinese speciality served with salad garnish and a choice of dip. The home-made soups, too, are a speciality. Half portions for children are available. There is a garden area; well-behaved dogs are admitted into the bar but not the lounge. The bar is best for walkers too – there is a flagged stone floor worn smooth by boots (both farm workers' and walkers' over the centuries.)

Telephone: 01789 840266.

How to get there: Wellesbourne is at the junction of the B4086 and the A429 about 6 miles south of Warwick. The Stag's Head is a short distance south of the bridge over the river Dene along the B4086.

Parking: The pub does not have a car park but there is plenty of road parking around Chestnut Square.

Length of the walk: 2½ miles. OS Map Landranger Series 151 Stratford-upon-Avon (inn GR 277552).

The walk takes you along the little, meandering river Dene to the hamlet of Walton. On the outward leg there are footpaths through the meadows passing Wellesbourne watermill. This is the centrepiece of a rural experience as there are gardens and nature trails, demonstrations of old crafts, home-made fare from the mill's own stoneground flour and a display of farm bygones. Past a ford the route goes to the estate hamlet of Walton – once allied to the great house of Walton Hall (now a hotel and country club). The return to the pub is along picturesque narrow lanes.

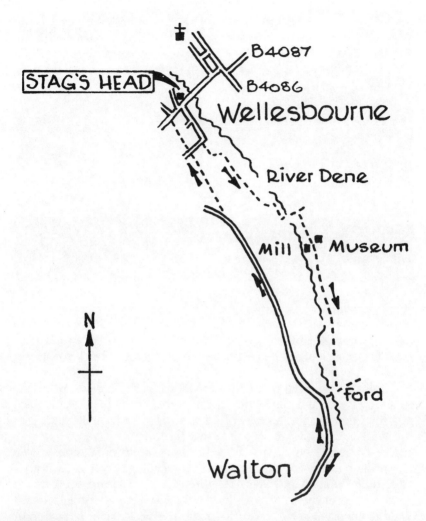

The Walk

Opposite the pub, walk along Chapel Lane to pass the Manor House, and the Old School House. After about 400 yards and by Baker's Hatch turn right along Lowes Lane. Within a step or two turn left down a signed footpath which leads to a kissing-gate into a pasture.

Follow the arrowed direction, keeping just to the left of an obsolete hedge marked by bushes. Go past posts to climb a stile at the very far end of the pasture. In the next field walk along the left-

Wellesbourne Mill.

hand border to a bridge over the river Dene. Turn left to a corner stile. Do not climb the stile but turn right along a track towards a farm.

Go through a metal gate and keep ahead (with barns on your left) to another gate and climb the stile alongside. Here is a vehicle track and the interesting watermill complex. Cross to a footpath signed to the Wildlife Garden. Climb a stile to a meadow.

Keep ahead – the path now borders the river. Climb a stile alongside a metal gate and maintain the heading. Climb a far corner stile, then another and keep the direction to a farm vehicle track. Turn right over the footbridge by the ford to a lane. Turn left to visit Walton, then when you want to begin the walk back, retrace your steps along the lane.

Continue on the lane and about ¾ mile past the ford take a signed path over a stile on the right. Follow the arrowed direction to a stile to a fenced way leading to a road. Cross to the footpath opposite. The path leads to another road. Chestnut Square and the Stag's Head are about 200 yards to the right.

Walton Hall.

Places of interest nearby

Wellesbourne airfield near the centre of the village was a wartime RAF aerodrome which trained bomber crews on Wellington aircraft. Today the site is a large industrial estate but the runways remain and there is some civilian flying and a small museum. However, of especial interest is the V-bomber which is visible from the road. The aircraft is being meticulously renovated and does make high speed ground runs.

Two miles along the B4086 Stratford Road is *Charlecote Park* with its deer park. The great house (built in 1558 in the shape of a letter 'E' to flatter the first Queen Elizabeth) was the seat of the Lucy family. Deer from the park are reputed to have been poached by Shakespeare. The place is now in the care of the National Trust.

⑯ Northend
The Red Lion

Northend was historically part of Burton Dassett, where there is a magnificent Norman church on a bleak, high hilltop. The houses of the village of Burton Dassett were along a rough lane running southwards from the church. The lords of the manor were the de Sudeleys, then the Botelers to be followed by the Belknaps. Sir Edward Belknap was something of a disaster. He enclosed 600 acres on the hills and evicted the 60 tenant farmers. This, together with the Black Death, depopulated the area. Northend is therefore relatively modern with many council houses built in the 1930s.

The Red Lion is now a freehouse – and it strikes the visitor as being very free and easy and just the place to unwind after a walk, with few restrictions for well-behaved dogs (or children). There is a bar where darts is enthusiastically played and a beamed lounge with exposed stonework and open fires in wintertime.

There are usually three real ales on offer at very competitive prices with Boddingtons and Tetley joined by a guest beer. There is draught Strongbow for the cider drinker. Meals at very reasonable prices are listed on a modest menu and the daily 'specials' are chalked on a board over the bar. These might include home-made chilli and rice, and filled jacket potatoes or Yorkshire puddings with a salad are often the first choice for walkers. There are always vegetarian dishes and children love the chicken nuggets (with chips and beans, of course).

The lunchtime opening hours are 12 noon to 3 pm every day. The evening hours are 7 pm to 11 pm (10.30 pm on Sundays). The pub sometimes opens all day especially in 'barbecue summertime'.

Telephone: 01295 770308.

How to get there: Northend lies about 10 miles south-east of Warwick. From the B4100 south of Gaydon, cross over the M40. The pub is in the centre of the village.

Parking: There is a car park at the front and side of the pub.

Length of the walk: 3 miles. OS Map Landranger series 151 Stratford-upon-Avon (inn GR 392525).

The Holy Well, Burton Dassett.

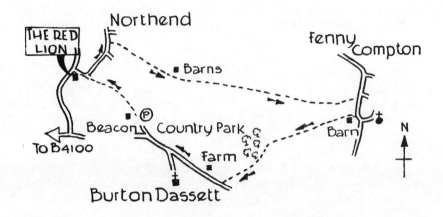

After a pleasant country ramble to Fenny Compton, the walk returns over the Burton Dassett Hills, which now comprise a country park. The botany and ecology have been fashioned by the disused ironstone quarries opened and closed since the middle of the 19th century. A signal station was once perched on the uplands; the present beacon tower replaced a much earlier structure. It was built by the rather despicable Sir Edward Belknap towards the end of the 14th century. Cromwell is said to have watched the progress of the battle of Edge Hill from this lofty and lovely viewpoint.

The Walk

Walk along the lane at the side of the pub. Go around one corner, then another. Nearing the end of the houses and opposite a residence called the White House (no, not that one!) take a signed path on the right.

Go along a vehicle track. At the end go through a metal gate to a pasture. Take the arrowed direction to turn left through a gateway. Again follow the arrowed way to cross the open field to pick up the line of a left-hand wire fence. At a corner maintain the old direction over the field.

Pass through a kissing-gate by a metal field gate. Bear left to go through a far corner gate. (Take care as the waymark may be a little awry!) Walk along a tractor way to pass by some black barns, then alongside a left-hand hedge.

Go over a railed bridge and maintain the direction through fields, aiming just to the left of a distant church spire. Climb a step stile adjoining a field gate and walk through a small meadow to climb another stile and continue to a road at Fenny Compton. The church here has an unusual dedication (to St Peter and St Clare).

Turn right on the road. Within 200 yards turn right down a vehicle drive signed as a bridleway. Go through a metal gate by a large barn. Follow the arrowed heading to cross a sheep pasture. Go through a metal gate to an often arable field. At once turn right. Follow the field boundary to gradually climb the hill. Go through a metal gate to sheep pastures. Follow a route to the left of the woods to join a tractor way. Pass through a metal gate.

Take the arrowed direction left, soon climbing alongside a left-hand wire fence to a gate to a lane. Turn right. Go over a cattle grid to the country park – magnificent views now with Edge Hill to the left and the battle site in the valley.

When you come to a road junction keep ahead (to the left is the 12th-century church of Burton Dassett, which has been called 'The Cathedral of the Hills'). Pass old quarry workings and again keep

The beacon tower.

ahead at the next junction towards the beacon tower (which may also have served as the tower of a windmill). By the tower leave the vehicle way. Bearing slightly left drop down the steep slope to a gate and a stile. The wide track is Mill Lane, the old route into Northend, and will bring you back to the Red Lion.

Places of interest nearby

Burton Dassett church is well worth a visit; a distinctive feature of the Norman building is the flight of 17 steps to reach the altar. Outside the church is the Holy Well – the well house dates from 1840.

Four miles south-west of Northend is *Edge Hill* where the Royalist troops were assembled prior to the great battle (the first of the Civil War) in 1642. A tower marks the spot where the King's standard was raised.

Three miles north-west is a fine *Motor Museum* on the site of the old RAF Gaydon airfield. The museum is open daily and contains a wide range of cars depicting the manufacture of British vehicles over the years. There are picnic facilities, restaurants and a children's playground.

Welford-on-Avon
The Shakespeare

Very little is known about the early life of William Shakespeare but there is a tale that he rather liked his ale. A rhyme about the villages in which he joined drinking contests at the local inn lists piping Pebworth, dancing Marston, haunted Hillborough, hungry Grafton, dodging Exhall, papist Wixford, beggarly Broom and drunken Bidford – but not a mention of Welford. His connections with the Shakespeare inn are therefore probably quite recent, a whim of the brewery with Stratford only a mile or so away. Local folk tell of the time when this was the baker's house, with ovens still in the out-houses. The change to a pub appears to have taken place in the last century.

The Shakespeare still has more the appearance of a 19th-century residence than licensed premises and the magnificent gardens add to this illusion. What once were living rooms have been added to the original small bar to create more space. By the bar the position of the old well can be detected from the hollow-sounding floor. An unusual feature is that the pub also serves as a library with over 600 books lining the shelves. Tourists and locals can freely take books and usually leave a volume in exchange. There is a children's section in the bar.

So while you are engrossed in that book what beers can you drink? The choice of well-kept real ales is between Wadworth 6X, Boddingtons Bitter, Whitbread's and Marston's Pedigree. For cider drinkers there is Weston's Stowford Press.

The menu is not vast but good, home-made, pub grub. There are always a few 'specials' chalked on the board and vegetarians can find something tasty to suit. The Shakespeare Grill is renowned – 4 oz gammon steak, 4 oz rump, a succulent lamb chop, sausage and black pudding plus all the trimmings – the walk perhaps should be after the feast! Children have a special list from which to choose – not only are all the dishes served with plenty of French fries but all come (perhaps later) with two free scoops of ice cream.

The hours at the Shakespeare are 11 am to 2.30 pm and 6 pm to 11 pm, Monday to Saturday. Sunday opening is from 12 noon to 3 pm and 7 pm to 10.30 pm.

Telephone: 01789 750443.

How to get there: Welford-on-Avon is about 3 miles south-west of Stratford along the B439. Turn left along a lane over the river. The pub is at the far end of the village down a road by the maypole.

Parking: There is a small car park beside the Shakespeare.

Length of the walk: 3 miles. OS Map Landranger Series 151 Stratford-upon-Avon (inn GR 150518).

The walk is through villages and along the valley of the tranquil river Avon. Over fields Weston-on-Avon is reached. This little, isolated place has a weatherworn 15th-century church and there is the base of an ancient cross. The route passes by delightful oft-photographed thatched cottages and another old place of worship at Welford. The Norman church of St Peter was built on a site associated with the Abbey of St Denis, Paris. The former mill (with two undershot wheels) is now a private house. Near the end of the walk is a tall maypole by a tree planted to commemorate the Silver Jubilee of King George V in 1935.

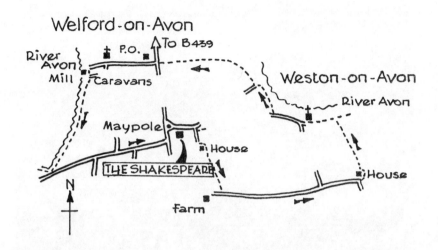

The Walk

From the small car park turn right on the road. Within 200 yards turn right down Pool Close. Ignoring a footpath arrow keep ahead to the end of the vehicle way. Go left as indicated then immediately regain the old heading to walk by a house (on the right).

At the end of the house garden go right into the next field. Again regain the original heading to continue to the far corner of the large field. Go through a hedge gap to a lane and turn left. Go past a road junction and 300 yards later (and just after the lane twists sharp right) go over a stile on the left. Walk at the side of a garden and pass an obsolete stile.

Continue to a squeeze stile in the far left-hand corner of a large sheep pasture. On a vehicle track turn left to pass by Weston-on-Avon church. Keep ahead at a junction and follow the cul-de-sac lane to the end. Turn right along a signed bridleway. The track soon borders the river then bears left alongside a tall wooden fence.

By the house drive of Witch Gate take a signed footpath on the right. Join a vehicle drive then at once leave it to keep ahead along a footpath which leads to a road by the green and post office at Welford. Cross to Church Street. Go by the church and cottages to the very end.

Bear left along a signed footpath and follow this to a vehicle way by Welford Mill. Go left then at once right to enter a caravan site. Walk to

Welford-on-Avon.

the far right-hand corner and climb the stile. There is now a clear track (part of the Avon Valley Pathway) which borders the river. After ½ mile climb a stile.

Leave the riverside to climb the bank left. Pass a seat and continue to a kissing-gate to a road. Turn left – there is a good view now over the vale. Drop down the hill to a T-junction at Welford. Go left, then right by the maypole to return to the Shakespeare.

Places of interest nearby

Three miles north-east of Welford-on-Avon along the B439 at Shottery is *Anne Hathaway's Cottage*. This thatched abode was the farmhouse home of Shakespeare's wife. Many romantic tales associated with the Bard are woven around this delightful cottage with its 'so-English' garden and orchard. The cottage is open daily.

Mary Arden's House is along lanes 4 miles north of Welford. This timber-framed house was the childhood home of Shakespeare's mother. Besides the house there is an interesting collection of old Warwickshire farming implements and country bygones. The house is open daily.

18 Lower Quinton
The College Arms

Henry VIII gave many lands around Quinton (originally called Queans-town in Old English) to Oxford's Magdalen College. Among the houses also in the gift were Magdalen House (which is now another pub, the Gay Dog) and the building which is now the College Arms. The College Arms was perhaps another farmhouse or, being so near, was used to house stonemasons building the nearby church.

'Lozengry Sable and Ermine and a chief Sable charged with three garden lilies proper' – so runs the heraldic description of the Arms of Magdalen College, the same arms which adorn the signpost of the pub.

This is a pub which has an old history but has been splendidly modernised. There is an old-fashioned bar with a stone-flagged floor which no doubt has welcomed farm workers' boots over many centuries but is just right for walking boots. Here is a dartboard and practical furnishings. The lounge is red carpeted and all the walls have exposed stonework. The large inglenook is hung with polished brass artefacts; the decorations over the bar are the garlands of hops which are a reminder of the excellent beers in this Whitbread house. The real ales are Boddingtons and Bass which are joined by two guest beers, such as the intriguing Scarlet Lady. The choice of draught cider is between Woodpecker and Scrumpy Jack. Children are welcome in the lounge if dining and dogs can visit the bar.

There is a wide range of food available from both the standard menu and the 'specials' board but this is a celebrated pub for gammon and egg suppers. There are more unusual dishes too, especially the 'starters': perhaps you will like the sound of liver, brandy and almond pâté or the Camembert and Brie in breadcrumbs. Vegetarians always have a good choice with the spinach and mushroom tagliatelli being very popular.

The opening hours are a little flexible but are generally 12 noon to 3 pm every day with the pub opening each evening from 7 pm. There is no garden but benches and tables are available at the front of the building.

Telephone: 01789 720342.

How to get there: 6 miles south-west of Stratford-upon-Avon along the B4632 turn left to the village of Lower Quinton. The pub is at the far end of the village near the church.

Parking: There is a car park at the side of the pub.

Length of the walk: 2½ miles. OS Map Landranger Series 151 Stratford-upon-Avon (inn GR 183472).

Lower Quinton is overlooked by the lovely green hump of Meon Hill which has an Iron Age fort perched on the 300 ft summit. The paths on the walk go halfway up the slopes to afford fine views over the Avon vale. Many legends are told about Meon but it was in 1945 that the upland became notorious when a farm worker was murdered with his own pitchfork on St Valentine's Day. The crime remains unsolved.

The Walk

Out of the car park turn left along the road. Pass a cottage with dipping thatch and then St Swithun's church (Saxon and Norman work in the building). Turn right – the path is signed through a gate

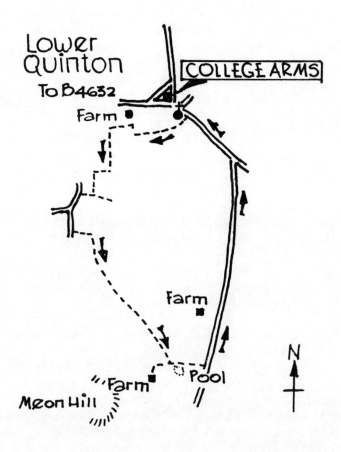

into the churchyard. Cross to a stile into a sheep pasture.

Bear slightly right to climb a stile in the far right-hand corner. Turn right for 50 yards, then left over another stile. Walk alongside a right-hand hedge. In a corner turn left. Within 75 yards climb a stile right then go immediately left to continue alongside a left-hand hedge.

Within 100 yards turn right over the open field to the opposite hedge corner. Turn left (with the hedge on the right side) to a farm vehicle track. Turn right to a road. Turn left on the road to the green at Upper Quinton. Take a lane left over the green. Keep ahead to a white house (Meon Cottage) then take a signed path left in front of the cottage. Climb a stile to a small pasture.

Cross to the opposite stile. Turn right at the side of a plantation. Climb a stile to a meadow. Take the arrowed direction to the far diagonal corner. Turn right over a stile. Walk alongside a left-hand hedge for 50 yards to climb a stile left. Walk beside a hedge then maintain the heading over the open field to a stile.

Cross a pasture to a stile to a farm drive. Turn left to pass a pool where ducks glide. At a lane turn left. Follow the lane to a T-junction. The College Arms is ¼ mile to the left.

Places of interest nearby

Stratford-upon-Avon and its many Shakespeare associations is only 4 miles distant. Holy Trinity church where the Bard is buried overlooks the river and the theatres have interesting tours backstage and displays of the intricate costumes of past productions.

There are pleasant riverside walks, boats to hire and ferries across the Avon. There are masses of swans and other wildfowl at Stratford just waiting to be fed by the tourists so do not forget the bits of bread! A special delight is to take a boat trip along the river – on one luxury craft it is possible to dine during the voyage.

There is a unique *Butterfly Farm* along Swan's Nest Lane just over the 15th-century Clopton Bridge. This is open daily and there are special family rates for entrance.

Between Lower Quinton and Stratford along the B4632 is the *Shire Horse Centre*. Besides the horses there are many farm animals to see and the springtime lambing season is especially popular with children. There are short walks, country displays and plenty of refreshment facilities. The centre is open daily with reduced rates and concessions.

19 **Whatcote**
The Royal Oak

This freehouse was built in 1168, like many other hostelries as an alehouse to cater for the workers who were building churches in the area. Thus it has been welcoming travellers for over 800 years.

Among these visitors were Cromwell and his officers who used the house as temporary quarters; it is said that the bread oven was removed and a hole for observation made in the wall facing Edge Hill where the royal troops were encamped. After the great battle it is recorded in Dugdale's *Antiquities of Warwickshire* that Cromwell and some of his followers came to the Royal Oak to slake their thirst.

Today, the ivy-covered pub gives a fine welcome in the snug bars; there is a huge inglenook fireplace (mind your head!) and plenty of settles and oak furniture. The brassware gleams and there is an interesting collection of old farm implements.

Families are welcome in the lounge which looks very cosy and inviting; well-behaved dogs too can follow their masters into the bar. There is no garden but you can sit at the benches and tables at the front of the pub and watch the world go by. The choice of real ales is between Bass and a guest beer (often Boddingtons). There is draught Strongbow for the cider drinkers and a full wine list including modestly priced house wines.

The food available includes a full English breakfast and there are many more delights listed in the menu and on the blackboard. Mine host is especially proud of the fresh trout. For vegetarians the vegetable moussaka and the crispy vegetable pancake are very popular.

Meals are available from 12 noon to 2 pm every day. In the evening the hours are 6 pm to 10 pm Monday to Saturday and 8 pm to 10 pm on Sunday. The drinking hours are 10.30 am to 3 pm and 6 pm to 11 pm Monday to Saturday and 12 noon to 3 pm and 7 pm to 10.30 pm on Sunday.

Telephone: 01295 680319.

How to get there: Whatcote is 4 miles north-east of Shipston on Stour. One mile north of Shipston along the A3400 turn right along lanes to the Royal Oak in the centre of the village.

Parking: There is a car park at the side of the pub.

Length of the walk: 3 miles. OS Map Landranger series 151 Stratford-upon-Avon (inn GR 300446).

St Peter's church in Whatcote is in lovely, lonely countryside but in 1940 it suffered damage by a direct hit from an enemy bomb. The Norman font was skilfully repaired but the building still shows the scars of war. Early on in the walk the woodlands of Hell Brake are passed; these are said to be haunted but in springtime they are a delight with carpets of bluebells. There are also deer in this area.

Idlicote is the other village visited. There is also a little church here which has the mark of the Norman masons but the idyllic spot is by the village pond.

The Walk

Turn right outside the Royal Oak to pass in front of the pub. As the road bends sharp right turn left down Church Lane. Within 150 yards turn right into the churchyard. Turn left (with an ancient preaching cross on the right) to pass through a gate.

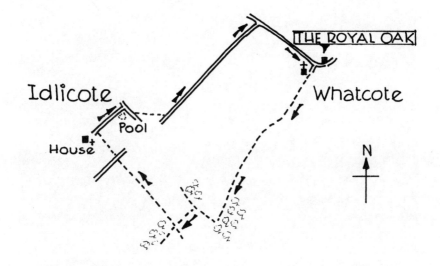

At once climb a stile and turn right alongside a fence. Near a corner go through a metal gate. Turn right then immediately left alongside a right-hand hedge. Climb a corner stile and maintain the old direction. Again there is a corner stile and we keep the same heading.

Near Hell Brake Wood go over a stile right. Turn left at the side of the wood. In the corner of the field turn right to a farm road. Turn left. At the next wood turn right (the wood is now on the left) then drop downhill alongside the hedge. Another left-hand wood is soon bordered. When this ends maintain the direction over the open field to a stile to a line.

Cross to the signed path opposite through a gate. Walk through the meadow along a clear track to a metal gate. Walk between the trees to a mansion drive. Idlicote's church is to the left but to continue the walk turn right to the village. Keep ahead then bear right by the pond.

Go past a thatched cottage. Just beyond turn left. The path is signed through a gate. Take the direction indicated to a stile to a lane. Turn left along the lane. At a T-junction turn right to return to Whatcote and the Royal Oak.

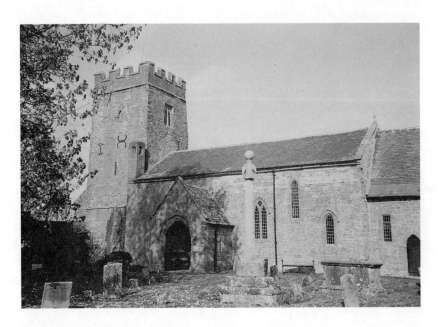

Whatcote church – hit by a bomb!

Places of interest nearby

Stratford-upon-Avon is 10 miles away from Whatcote. Besides its many associations with Shakespeare there is also a Teddy Bear Museum and a Butterfly Farm, both of which are open daily. Children also love to visit the Rosie and Jim shop in Guild Street.

The *Stratford Canal* comes into the town and a lock joins it to the River Avon Navigation so this is a mecca for canal craft and a great gathering place for swans and other waterfowl.

Seven miles north-east of Whatcote is *Edge Hill*. The site of the first battle of the Civil War (1642) is on War Department land and closed to the public but Edge Hill where the Royalists raised their standard is a lofty viewpoint.

⟨20⟩ Long Compton
The Red Lion Hotel

Since the construction of the M40, the passing traffic in Long Compton has greatly decreased and the village inn has had to rely even more on its long respected reputation. That it has succeeded is evidenced by the popularity of this freehouse.

Although the hostelry dates from the 16th century when it was a coaching inn on the toll road from the Midlands to Oxford, it skilfully blends the old world charm of heavy oak-beamed low ceilings, open fireplaces, exposed stonework and many cosy corners with modern facilities which today's visitors (and especially ramblers!) expect. For a long period the place was owned by the family of the Marquis of Northampton whose seat is at Compton Wynyates.

Many locals talk with affection of Aunt Phoebe who held the licence during the first three decades of the century. Her generosity included the gift of the fine playing field to Long Compton. Some even suggest she is a friendly ghost at the inn but as is usual with these happenings nothing can be verified!

The Lychgate at Long Compton church.

This is an ideal pub for all the family; there is a family room with a pool table and outside, a lovely garden with a splendid play area. In the inviting bar there are many conversation stimulants, such as the array of old bottles and the photographs of the village football team dating back to 1894. Darts, too, is popular here.

There is a good choice of real ales including John Smith's, Ruddles, Webster's and Old Speckled Hen. The draught cider is Bulmer's Traditional. There is an excellent wine list especially featuring French wines – which is very welcome if you dine in the intimate atmosphere of the candle-lit restaurant.

If you have to make do with a bar meal do not despair – there is a fine range of food listed on the Chef's Specials board and the Bar Bistro menu. There are all the old favourites including lasagne, chilli con carne and steak and kidney pie but you may also find the 'Sizzlers' – massive steaks, tandoori chicken or chilli prawns. Children have the choice from fish fingers, sausages or chicken nuggets – all with the inevitable basket of chips, of course.

The opening hours are Monday to Saturday 11 am to 2.30 pm and 6 pm to 11 pm in the evening. The reduced Sunday opening is from 12 noon to 3 pm (when a traditional Sunday lunch is available) and from 7 pm to 10.30 pm.

Telephone: 01608 684221.

How to get there: Long Compton is on the A3400 road between Shipston on Stour and Chipping Norton. The inn is on the main road at the very south end of the village.

Parking: There is a large car park at the side and rear of the pub.

Length of the walk: 3 miles. OS Map Landranger Series 151 Stratford-upon-Avon (inn GR 289324).

The route starts by taking you almost the length of this pretty village. Look out for the thatched cottages, the old smithy (now a private house), the base of the ancient village cross and the unusual lychgate in front of the 13th-century church. The lychgate was once a cottage, with the bottom storey removed. Away from the village is some of the most attractive scenery in Warwickshire with lovely views over the Cotswolds.

The Walk

Out of the car park of the pub turn left along the A3400. Pass the ancient cross and the church with its lychgate. As the main road twists sharp left at a road junction at the end of the village, turn right down a vehicle drive which is signed as a footpath.

Go through a metal gate into a sheep pasture and walk to the left of a pool and willows. Pass through another metal gate to join a wide cart track. This leads into a field. Keep ahead at the side of the field. Pass through another gate then walk alongside a left-hand wood. In the far corner climb a step stile.

Still on the same direction, walk along a wide track through a wood of tall poplars. There is a sharp climb to a T-junction of tracks. Turn right along a forester's road which gradually climbs to the top of the ridge along a way scented by bluebells in springtime.

Out of the woodlands continue along a broad track with woods now on the left-hand side. Keep ahead at a junction of tracks. When a right-hand hedge is met turn right to continue with this hedge on

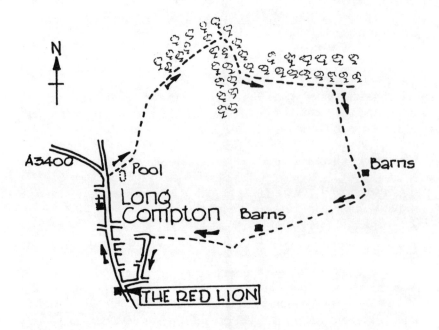

your right-hand side.

When the hedge ends keep ahead along a clear bridleway. There are glorious vistas now with the Rollright Stones and King's Stone on the far hills. Pick up the line of a right-hand wire fence. Past some old barns (on the left) drop down a rutted track to join another farm road. Continue along this way to pass more barns.

When a lane is reached through a gate turn left. Keep ahead at a junction to reach a T-junction by a farm. Turn right to the A3400 and the Red Lion is just to the left.

The base of the ancient cross at Long Compton.

Places of interest nearby

On the ridge above *Long Compton* are many historical stones. On one side of the road is the solitary King's Stone. Legends say that a king who set out to conquer England was transformed into a stone by a witch.

On the other side of the road are the stones called The Whispering Knights – they suffered the same fate as their monarch. Not far distant is the best preserved stone circle in the Midlands. Much has been written about the boulders but the mystery as to their real history remains.

Ten miles north-west is *Chipping Campden* with its splendid 'wool' church. It is here that the 100-mile pathway of the Cotswold Way starts.